I Have a Date! Now What?

From
'One-and-Done'
to
'This might actually last!"

By
J.R. Mays

Word Inventions
Corvallis, Oregon

Word Inventions--
inventwithwords.com
Copyright 2022 by J.R. Mays

ISBN # 9780976563280

Personal significance #'s:
9…or 4.

Introduction:

I've written this book for those who want (or need) to chuckle at the dating life or--since their own has achieved a level of perfection unsurpassed in human history---the dating life of other folks.

It might also appeal to readers who need a good cry...at all the goofs and gaffes they've contributed to the vast archives of dating misery. (Disclaimer: The author has *NEVER* experienced any such misery.)

How to use *I Have a Date, Now What?*

— Tweet out/post your newfound 'wisdom'.

— Gift a friend with a copy. (Make sure you do it ASAP before it hits the best seller list. Who knows--it might even qualify you as an 'influencer'.)

— Bring it on your next date. (Team up to avoid—or, for you risk-takers, reenact—the pitfalls highlighted in the book. Why not include one of the 'date escape' tips to close out the evening?)

— Use *I Have a Date's* hints and warnings to set up a 'world's worst date' party. (I still shudder at my page on manscaping.)
Enjoy!

Here goes...

Dating hang-ups?
Try fear aversion therapy.

Forget the script...
It's just a date.

Odds are the rumor mill will kick in long before you even meet up.

Let'em talk.

Let's deflate
that ego a bit
before your first date.

Save yourself the anguish.
Just assume he'll be late.

And if
he pulls a no-show?
Keep your faithful
Plan B sidekick nearby.

Pre-date recon--yes!
His tie-dyed muscle shirt
might steer you
toward 'casual chic'.

Shyness is one thing.
But a fashion theme?
Meh.

'Pick me up at work!'
Not always the best idea.

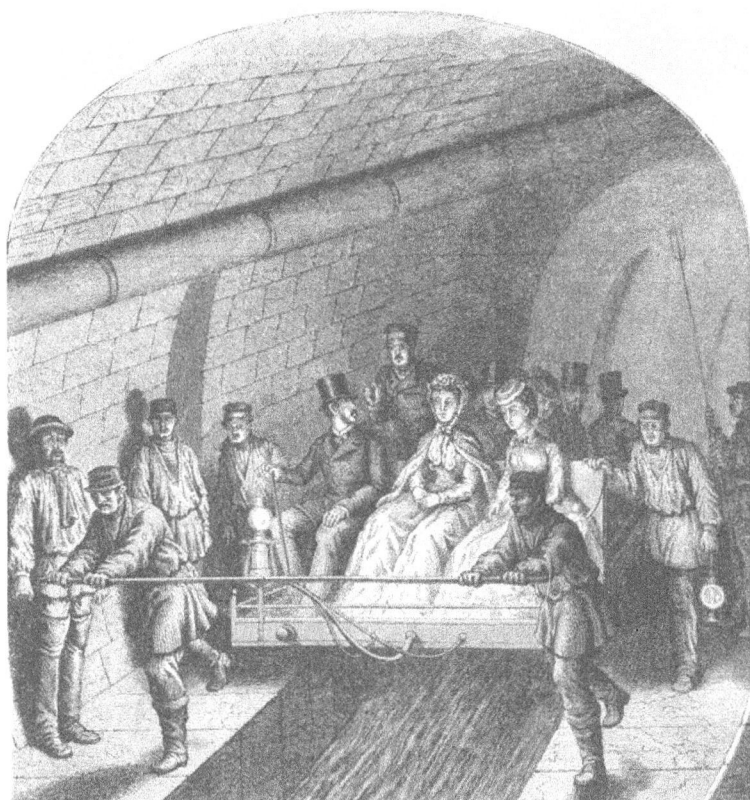

Make sure your date's
definition of 'rideshare'
matches yours.

Too much talk of
'high school heroics'?
At least give
the occasional nod.

A questionable tactic
if things don't
go your way.

Some special talents
might need to be kept
under wraps.

Meeting his friends
for the first time?
Plan on a few moments
'under the microscope'.

Yes, dates can go bad.
But try keeping
your hideout
in the building.

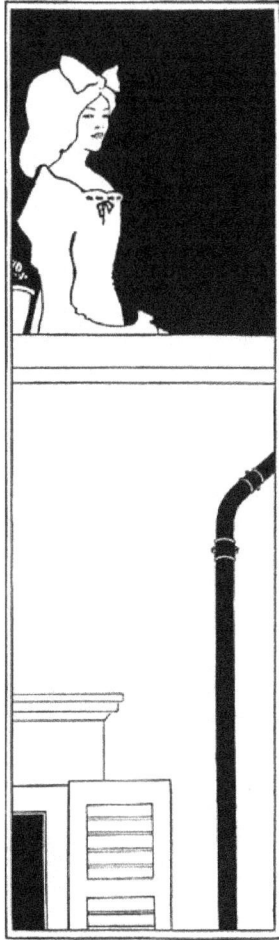

Another escape option...
just make sure the pipe
is secure.
(and you've done some stretching)

Let's all just take a breath.

One can handle only so much wisdom in one sitting.

Okay, Round 2

If a love potion's
your answer,
it's time to re-strategize.

Maybe there is something to that manscaping thing.

Don't rule out plastic surgery either.

You know what they say
about first impressions...
or do you?

'Am I late?'
Not the ideal
opening line here.
Read your cues.

Meeting the family
on that first date?
Bold.
And risky.

Expect at least
one scary relative
who lives to humiliate.

Just in case,
steer clear of
her ex's house.

Just say no
to 'quick'
pre-date stop-offs.

It's a date,
not a
locker room session.

If only
you'd stuck with
your ab workouts…

Dating straight from work?
A bit off-putting.
At times, just plain creepy.

It says 'animal lover'
on her dating profile.
Set a few limits
ahead of time.

Perhaps the best reason
to meet at a neutral site.

Walking in the rain--
not always
the romantic boost
you'd hoped for.

BUT...
if they predict rain,
the umbrella may well be
your best friend.

There's 'manly'
There's even 'macho'.
But...
stop short of 'Neanderthal'.

Take note of subtle hints
that your date wants
to call it a night.

Just assume it was
something you said...
or did...
or didn't say...
or didn't do.

Because it probably was.

You called her Jane.
She's Megan.
Your pants split.
You know where.
You clipped her heel.
And sent her flying.
Someday you'll laugh...
Someday.

THE END

The dating scene awaits.

Major fails at introductions...

Introduction Version #1: So, here's my book of dating advice. Revel in its wisdom.

Introduction Version #2: Welcome to this expertly crafted book. It is brimming with wisdom and advice that will carry you from that awkward first date all the way to the altar. The author denies culpability for any developments beyond that blessed day, however. 'Date Nights' that occur during marriage are the partners' own responsibility.

Introduction Version #3: Sorry if this introduction is a bit scattered, as I'm also crafting my Pulitzer Prize acceptance speeches [multiple categories] and my Nobel Prize [for this book's historic contributions to world peace]. Final point: I request that you not send personal checks of appreciation for how much this book has enhanced your life. Just knowing your credit card information is enough.

--JR Mays

Disclaimer:
This introduction is a work of fiction teeming with exaggeration, hyperbole, and redundancy. Names, characters, places, and incidents either are products of the author's imagination or are used fictitiously, including the misconception that he thinks this book will sell.

THIS MUCH IS TRUE, HOWEVER.
ALL ILLUSTRATIONS ARE IN THE PUBLIC DOMAIN AND I FOUND THEM AT

OLDBOOKILLUSTRATIONS.COM.

TREAT YOURSELF TO TONS OF FUN IMAGES
AND VISIT THAT SITE.

J.R. Mays is equally qualified to dole out advice on dating, brain surgery, and Mars landings. When he isn't writing, baking, or catering to his dog's every whim, he's busy setting fashion trends (with the added benefit of creeping out the local Neighborhood Watch).

www.ingramcontent.com/pod-product-compliance
Lightning Source LLC
Chambersburg PA
CBHW050951030426
42339CB00007B/377